learn to draw
Military Machines

Step-by-step instructions for more than 25 high-powered vehicles

ILLUSTRATED BY TOM LAPADULA

This library edition published in 2016 by Walter Foster Jr.,
an imprint of Quarto Publishing Group USA Inc.
6 Orchard Road, Suite 100
Lake Forest, CA 92630

Distributed in the United States and Canada by
Lerner Publisher Services
241 First Avenue North
Minneapolis, MN 55401 U.S.A.
www.lernerbooks.com

First Library Edition

Library of Congress Cataloging-in-Publication Data

Learn to draw military machines : step-by-step instructions for more than 25 high-powered
vehicles / Illustrated by Tom LaPadula. -- First Library Edition.
      pages cm
 Includes bibliographical references and index.
 ISBN 978-1-939581-98-3 (alk. paper)
1. Vehicles, Military, in art--Juvenile literature. 2. Drawing--Technique--Juvenile literature.
I. LaPadula, Tom, illustrator.
  NC825.M54L43 2016
  743'.8962--dc23

                                                                              2015034446

9 8 7 6 5 4 3 2 1

Table of Contents

Tools & Materials 4

How to Use This Book 5

Military Basics 6

Military Machines 7

Twin-Engine Attack Helicopter 8

Military Transport Aircraft 10

Airborne Warning & Control System (AWACS) 12

Vertical/Short Takeoff & Landing Aircraft 14

B-52 Bomber 16

Black Hawk Twin-Engine Helicopter 18

M1 Abrams Battle Tank 20

Stealth Ship 22

Amphibious Armored Car 24

M113 Family of Vehicles 26

Tandem-Rotor Heavy-Lift Helicopter 28

Armored Combat Vehicle 30

Four-Wheel-Drive Utility Vehicle 32

M36 Tank Destroyer 34

F-16 36

Lightweight Twin-Engine Helicopter 38

Twin-Engine Military Hovercraft 40

Medium-Lift Transport Helicopter 42

High Mobility Multipurpose Wheeled Vehicle (HMMWV) . . . 44

Stealth Fighter Jet 46

F-14 48

Guided Missile Submarine 50

Tilt-Rotor Vertical/Short Takeoff & Landing Aircraft . . . 52

Maritime Patrol Aircraft 54

Nuclear-Powered Supercarrier 56

Heavy Expanded Mobility Tactical Truck (HEMTT) 58

Research Vessel 60

Search and Rescue (SAR) Helicopter 62

Mini Quiz Answers 64

Tools & Materials

There's more than one way to bring military machines to life on paper—you can use crayons, markers, colored pencils, or even paints. Just be sure you have plenty of good military colors—greens, grays, and browns.

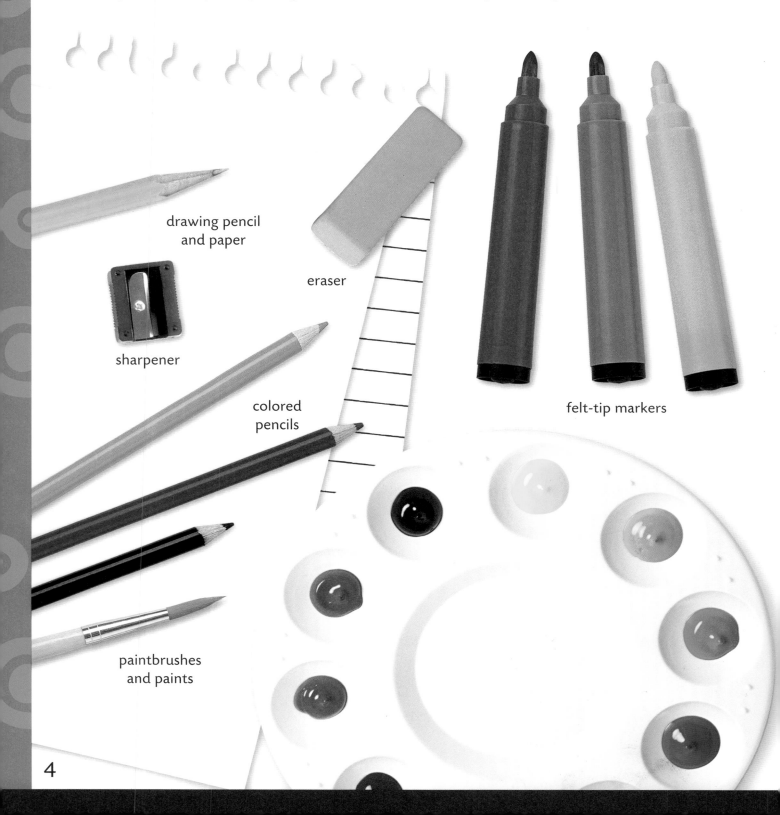

drawing pencil
and paper

eraser

sharpener

colored
pencils

felt-tip markers

paintbrushes
and paints

How to Use This Book

The drawings in this book are made up of basic shapes, such as circles, triangles, and rectangles. Practice drawing the shapes below.

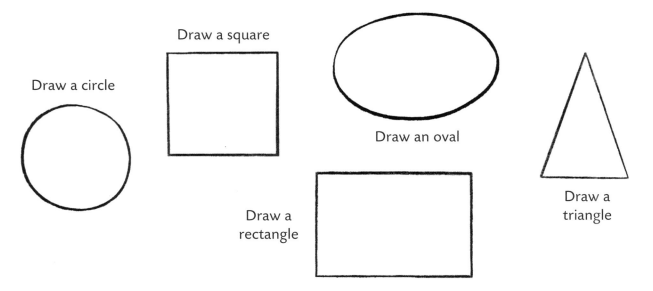

Draw a square

Draw a circle

Draw an oval

Draw a rectangle

Draw a triangle

Notice how these drawings begin with basic shapes.

In this book, you'll learn about the size, weight, fuel capacity, and speed of each featured military vehicle. Look for mini quizzes along the way to learn new and interesting facts!

Look for this symbol, and check your answers on page 64!

Military Basics

Most countries divide their military into three basic branches: army, navy, and air force. Each branch has different responsibilities, so they use different machines that help them successfully complete their missions.

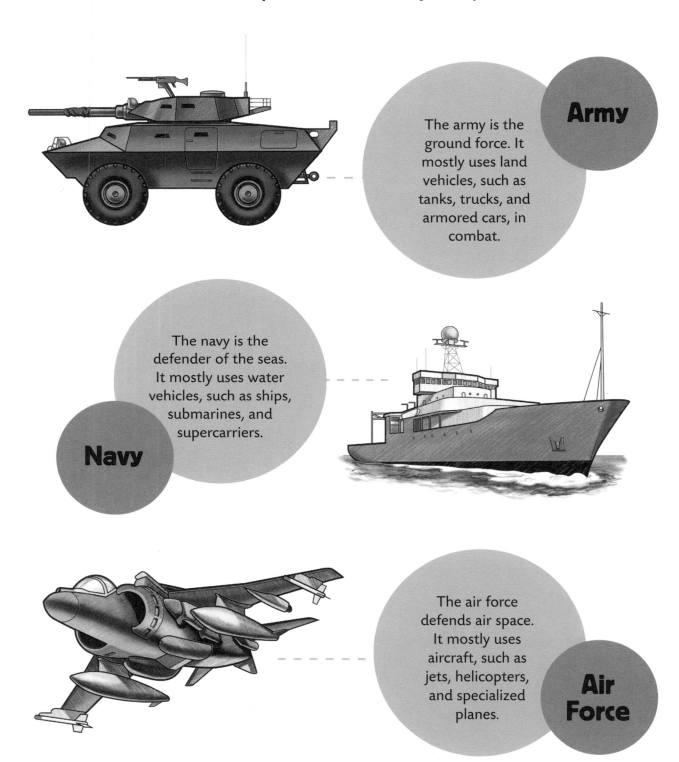

Army

The army is the ground force. It mostly uses land vehicles, such as tanks, trucks, and armored cars, in combat.

Navy

The navy is the defender of the seas. It mostly uses water vehicles, such as ships, submarines, and supercarriers.

Air Force

The air force defends air space. It mostly uses aircraft, such as jets, helicopters, and specialized planes.

Military Machines

Military machines are high powered, high performing, and massive!
Take a look at the specifications of an average car to compare.

Average car

Size:
14 to 16 feet long
Weight:
3,000 to 4,000 pounds
Fuel capacity:
About 16 gallons
Speed:
120 to 150 mph
maximum

Helicopter

Size:
98 feet long
Weight:
23,400 pounds
Fuel Capacity:
1,034 gallons
Speed:
196 mph

Tank

Size:
32 feet long
Weight:
56 tons
Fuel Capacity:
498 gallons
Speed:
42 mph

Fun Fact!

The military branches also provide support to each other during combat missions. For example, the air force provides air support to the army on the ground, and the navy provides aircraft carriers and runways for the air force.

Twin-Engine Attack Helicopter

Details

Size: 58 feet long
Weight: 10,000 to 12,000 pounds
Fuel Capacity: 412 gallons
Speed: 200 mph

Did You Know?

The twin-engine attack helicopter's climb rate is about 27 feet per second.

A power-packed chopper with a chain gun and rockets, this aircraft is designed for close-combat missions.

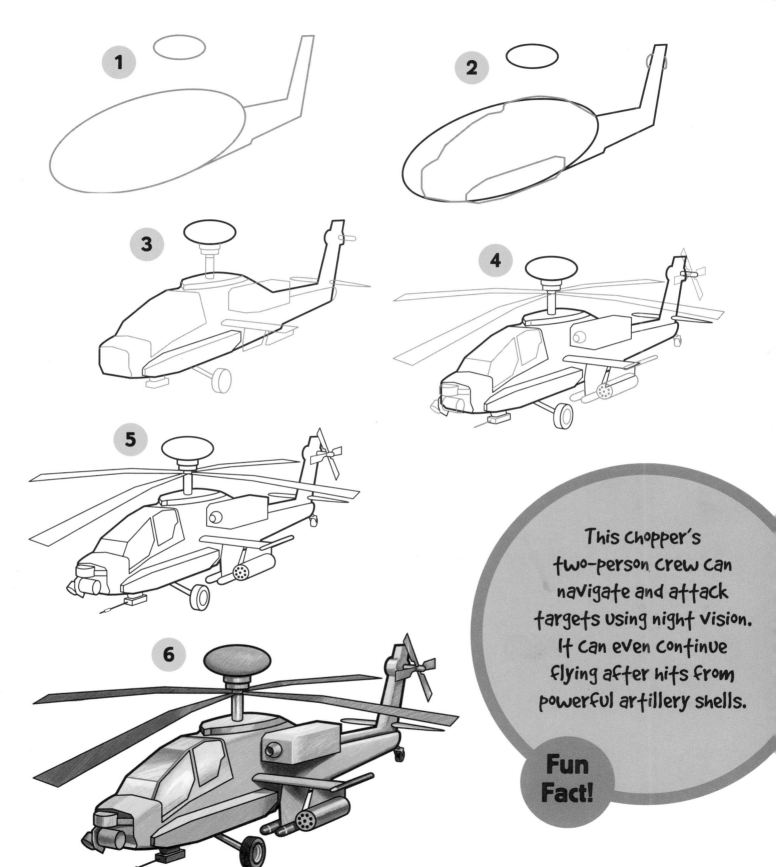

This chopper's two-person crew can navigate and attack targets using night vision. It can even continue flying after hits from powerful artillery shells.

Fun Fact!

Military Transport Aircraft

Despite its large size, this aircraft is designed to land on short runways quickly and efficiently. A three-person crew helps load cargo and troops through a rear ramp. Tanks and trucks simply drive right into it!

Fun Fact!

Weight: 277,000 pounds

Speed: About 515 mph

Fuel Capacity: 28,000 gallons

Size: 174 feet long

This plane carries troops and equipment thousands of miles across the ocean. It can haul up to 500,000 pounds!

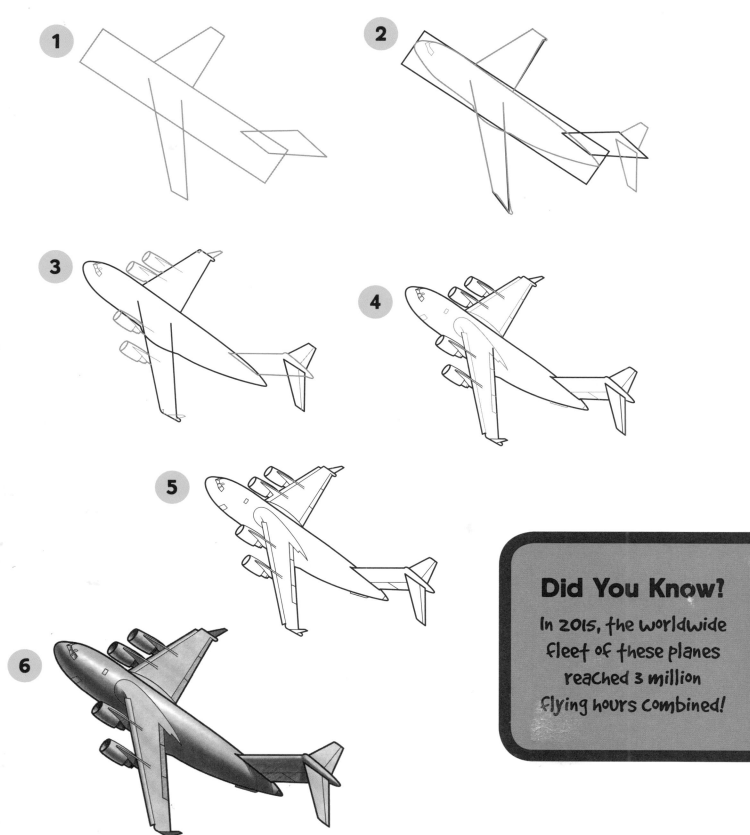

Did You Know?

In 2015, the worldwide fleet of these planes reached 3 million flying hours combined!

Airborne Warning & Control System

Details

Size: 152 feet, 11 inches long
Weight: 205,000 pounds
Fuel Capacity: 21,000 gallons
Speed: 530 mph

Did You Know?

The radar dish, or rotodome, is 30 feet in diameter and 6 feet thick at the center.

An AWACS is a radar dish covered in a special damage-resistant case that attaches to the top of an aircraft.

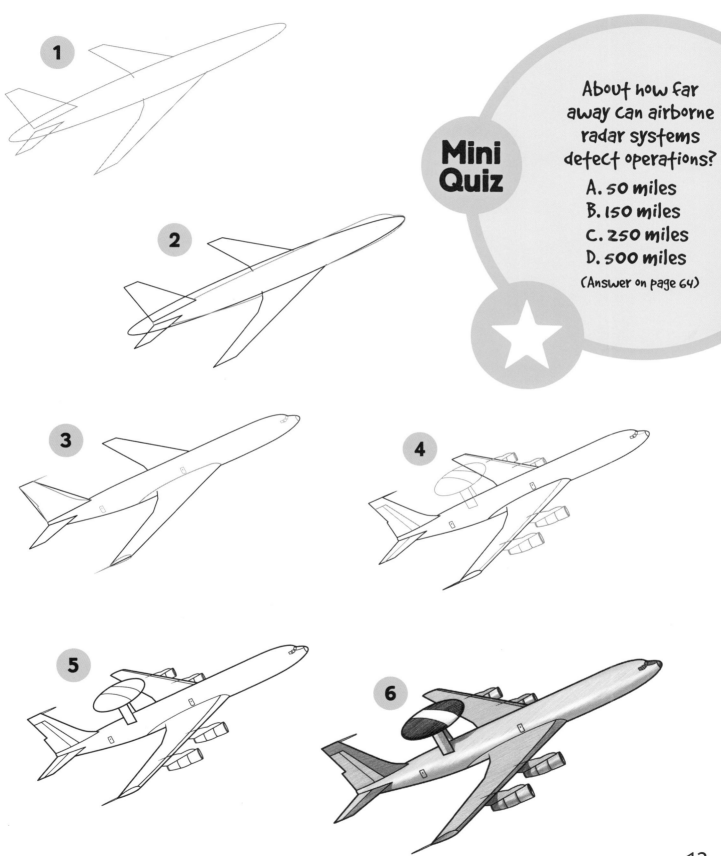

Mini Quiz

About how far away can airborne radar systems detect operations?

A. 50 miles
B. 150 miles
C. 250 miles
D. 500 miles

(Answer on page 64)

Vertical/Short Takeoff & Landing Aircraft

Weight:
10,000 to 14,000 pounds

Size:
42 to 47 feet long

Speed:
545 to 735 mph

Fuel Capacity:
About 1,100 gallons with the ability to hold external tanks

Did You Know?

There are several different kinds of vertical/short takeoff and landing aircraft. The most famous is the Harrier Jump Jet, which was developed by the British.

**This may look like a normal jet, but it's full of surprises—
it can take off and land just like a helicopter.**

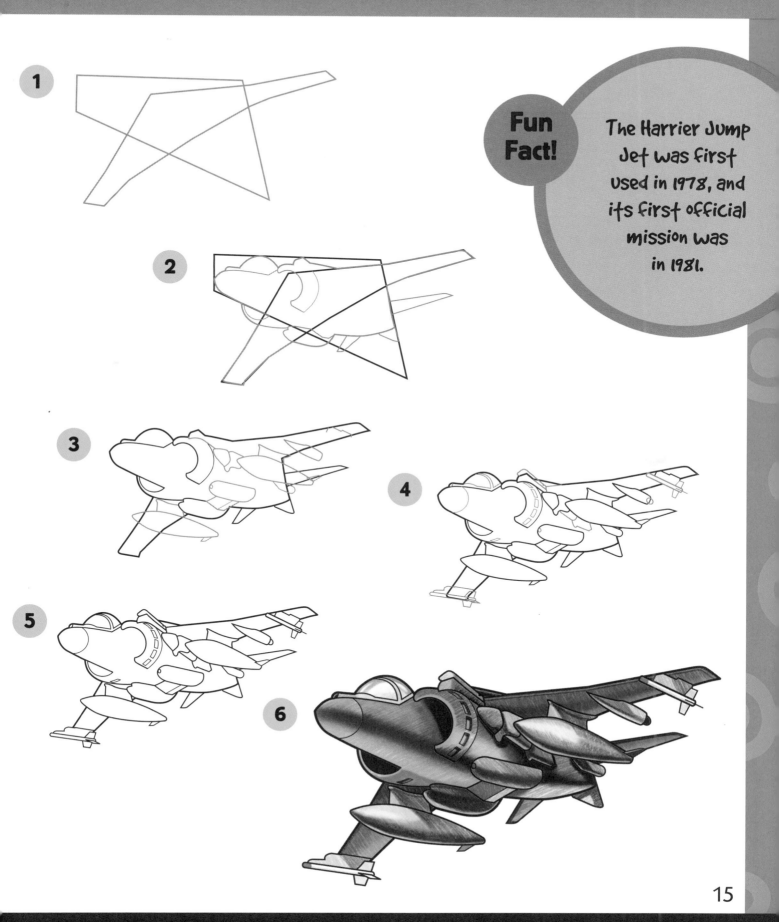

Fun Fact!

The Harrier Jump Jet was first used in 1978, and its first official mission was in 1981.

B-52 Bomber

Fuel Capacity:
48,000 gallons

Weight:
185,000 pounds

Speed:
650 mph

Size: 159 feet,
4 inches long

Did You Know?

The B-52 is smart! The B-52 uses the same avionics computer as the space shuttle!

Powered by eight turbo-jet engines, this behemoth bomber was first introduced in 1952 and isn't due for retirement until 2040!

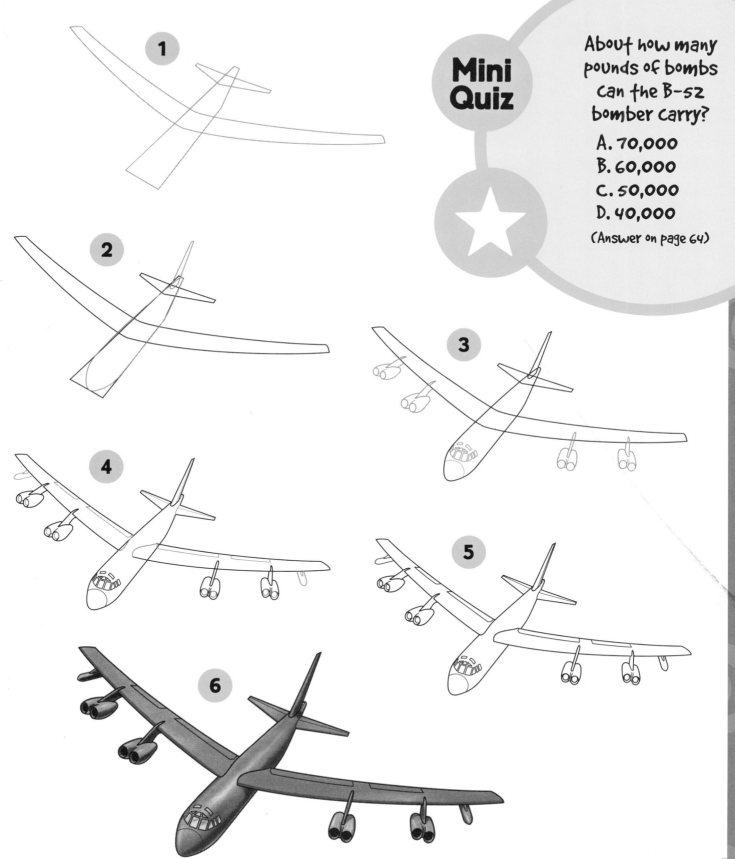

Mini Quiz

About how many pounds of bombs can the B-52 bomber carry?

A. 70,000
B. 60,000
C. 50,000
D. 40,000

(Answer on page 64)

Black Hawk Twin-Engine Helicopter

Details

Size: 64 feet,
10 inches long
Weight: 10,000 to
12,000 pounds
Fuel Capacity: 360 gallons
with the ability to hold
external tanks
Speed: 150 to 200 mph

Did You Know?

Multifaceted war machines, Black Hawks have two machine guns fitted to their doors and can withstand hits from heavy artillery.

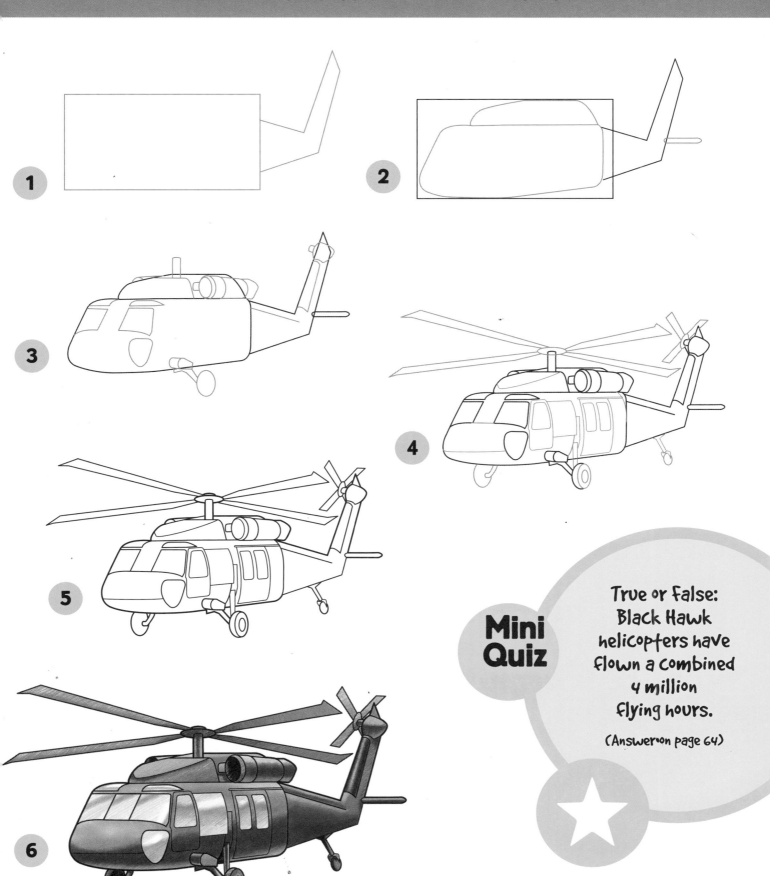

Mini Quiz

True or False: Black Hawk helicopters have flown a combined 4 million flying hours.

(Answer on page 64)

M1 Abrams Battle Tank

Did You Know?

This tank is named after the late General Creighton W. Abrams, who was the Army Chief of Staff from 1972 to 1974.

Weight: 60 tons
Speed: 45 mph
Size: 32 feet long
Fuel Capacity: 498 gallons

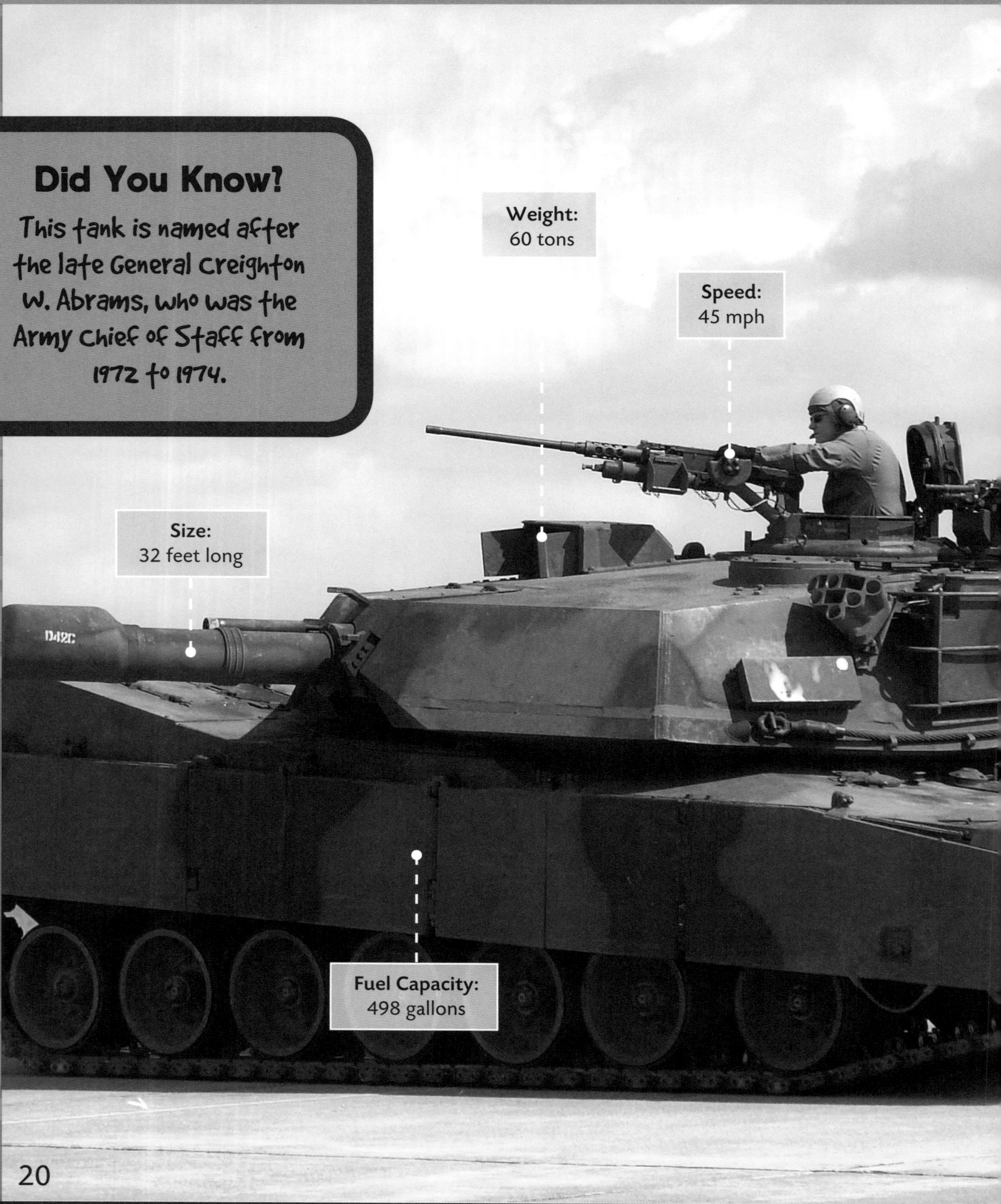

A 1,500-horsepower engine, three machine guns, and a 120mm smoothbore cannon make this tank one tough trooper!

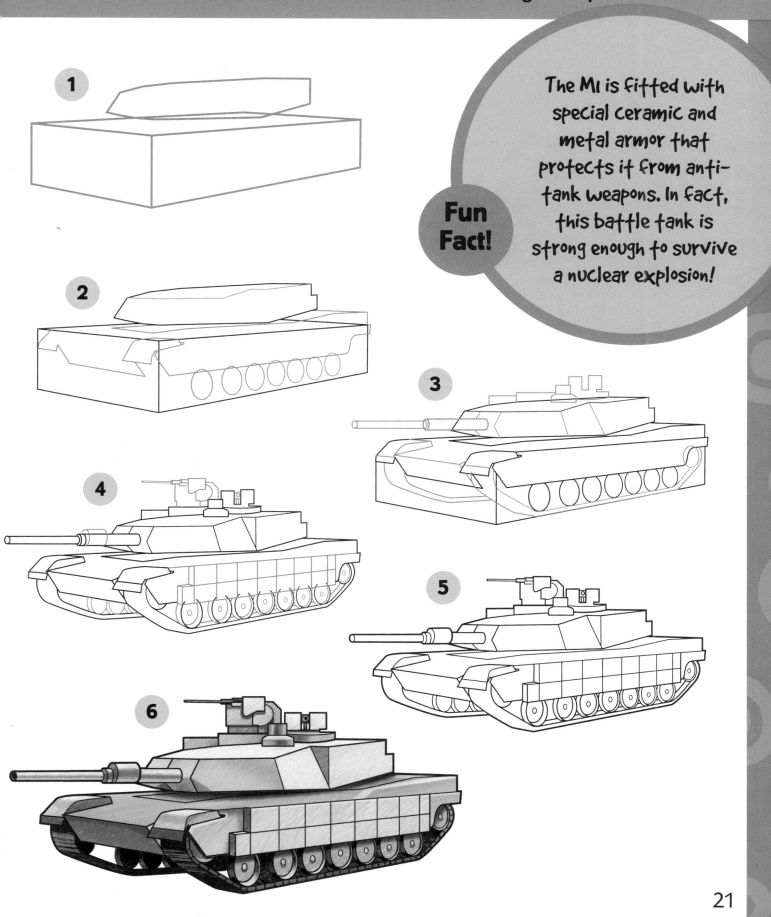

Fun Fact!

The M1 is fitted with special ceramic and metal armor that protects it from anti-tank weapons. In fact, this battle tank is strong enough to survive a nuclear explosion!

Stealth Ship

Did You Know?

The Sea Shadow was retired and dismantled in 2012.

Weight:
Over 500 tons

Speed:
15 mph

Size:
164 feet long

The Sea Shadow, one of many types of stealth ships, hid from radar detection thanks to its unique shape.

Mini Quiz

How much did it cost to build the Sea Shadow?

A. 15 million dollars
B. 25 million dollars
C. 50 million dollars
D. 100 million dollars

(Answer on page 64)

Amphibious Armored Car

Details

Size: 18 feet, 7 inches long
Weight: 16,250 pounds
Fuel Capacity: 80 gallons
Speed: 60 mph

Did You Know?

While this vehicle can drive through water, it can't go very fast! Its maximum speed in water is only 3 mph.

This multi-use car is "amphibious" because it travels across both rivers and battlefields with ease. It's used as an ambulance, anti-tank vehicle, and troop carrier.

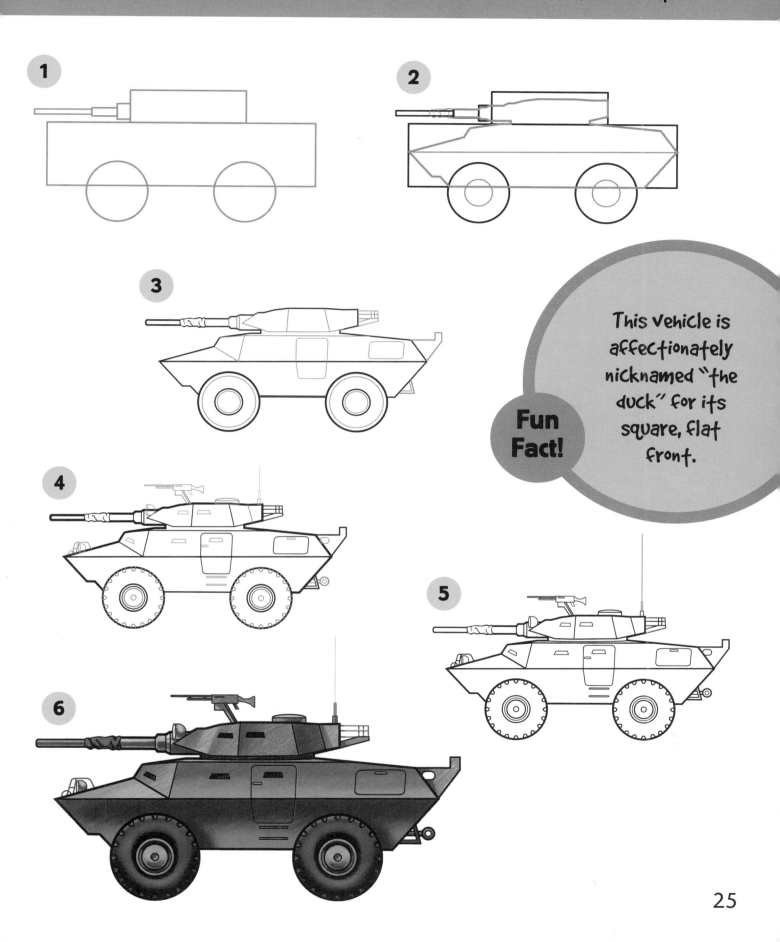

Fun Fact!

This vehicle is affectionately nicknamed "the duck" for its square, flat front.

M113 Family of Vehicles

Did You Know?

The M113 family of vehicles is made of 12 different models that are used in a variety of combat roles.

Weight:
20,310 to
23,575 pounds

Speed:
37 to 41 mph

Size:
16 feet long

Fuel Capacity:
95 gallons

The M113 is the most popular armored vehicle in the world. About 80,000 are used in more than 50 countries!

1

2

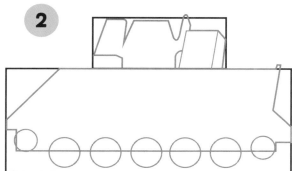

3

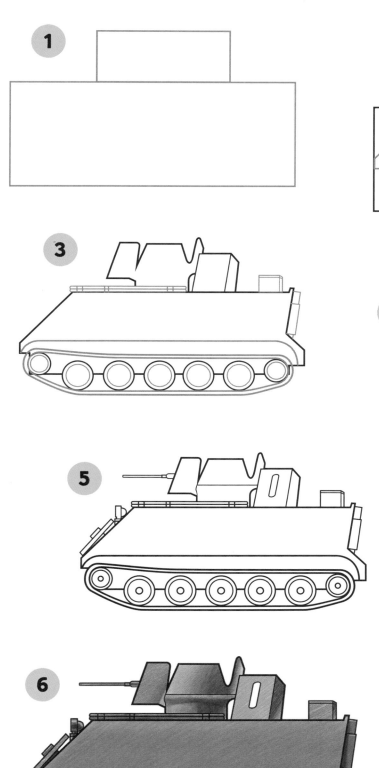

4

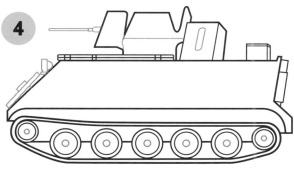

5

6

Mini Quiz

How many people can the M113 carry?

A. 8
B. 13
C. 15
D. 20

(Answer on page 64)

Tandem-Rotor Heavy-Lift Helicopter

Weight:
23,400 pounds

Fuel Capacity:
1,034 gallons

Speed:
196 mph

Did You Know?

This muscular helicopter is very strong. Three cargo hooks attached to its underside allow it to haul up to 26,000 pounds!

Size:
98 feet,
10 inches long

This combat helicopter can transport 44 soldiers and travel more than 330 miles in a single trip.

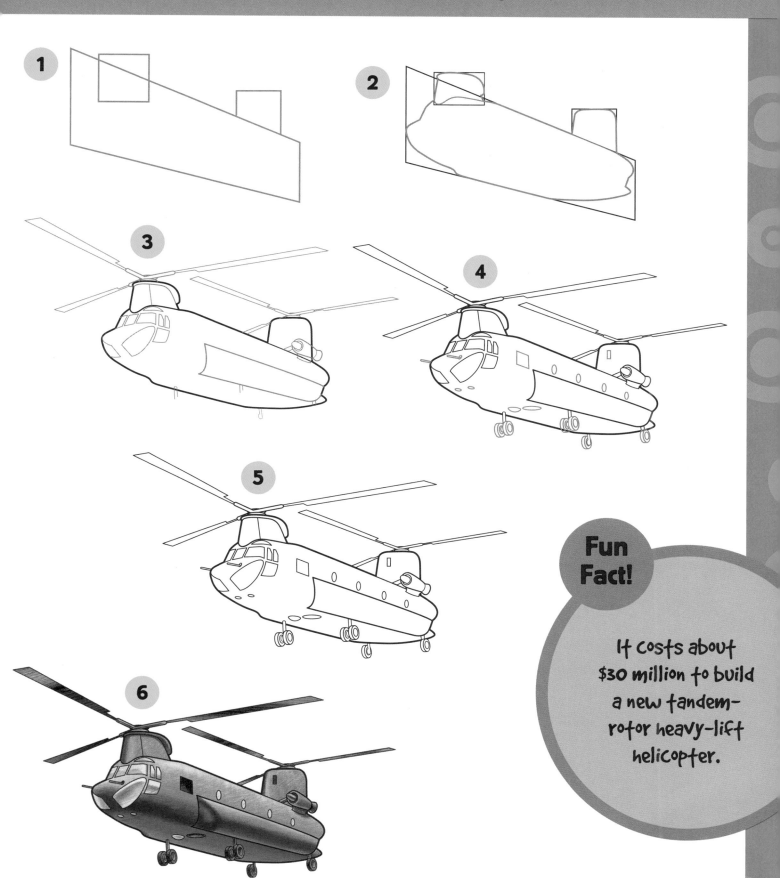

Fun Fact!

It costs about $30 million to build a new tandem-rotor heavy-lift helicopter.

Armored Combat Vehicle

Did You Know?

This vehicle has the ability to shift from four-wheel drive for highway driving to eight-wheel drive for cross-country driving.

This mean fighting machine is packed with heavy-duty weapons and wrapped in a rough-and-tough armor.

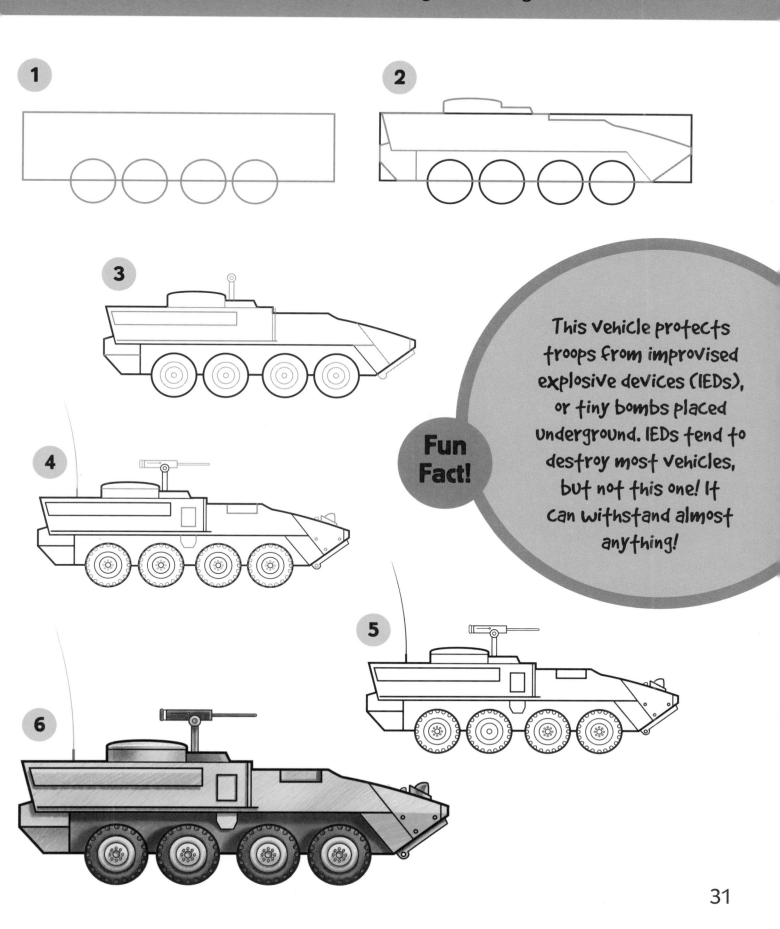

Fun Fact!

This vehicle protects troops from improvised explosive devices (IEDs), or tiny bombs placed underground. IEDs tend to destroy most vehicles, but not this one! It can withstand almost anything!

Four-Wheel-Drive Utility Vehicle

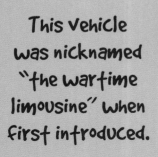

Fun Fact!

This vehicle was nicknamed "the wartime limousine" when first introduced.

Size:
11.5 feet long

Weight:
2,500 to 3,500 pounds

Fuel Capacity:
15 to 17 gallons

Speed:
65 mph

This open-air vehicle was the United States Military's go-to truck for decades. It was retired from duty in the mid-1980s.

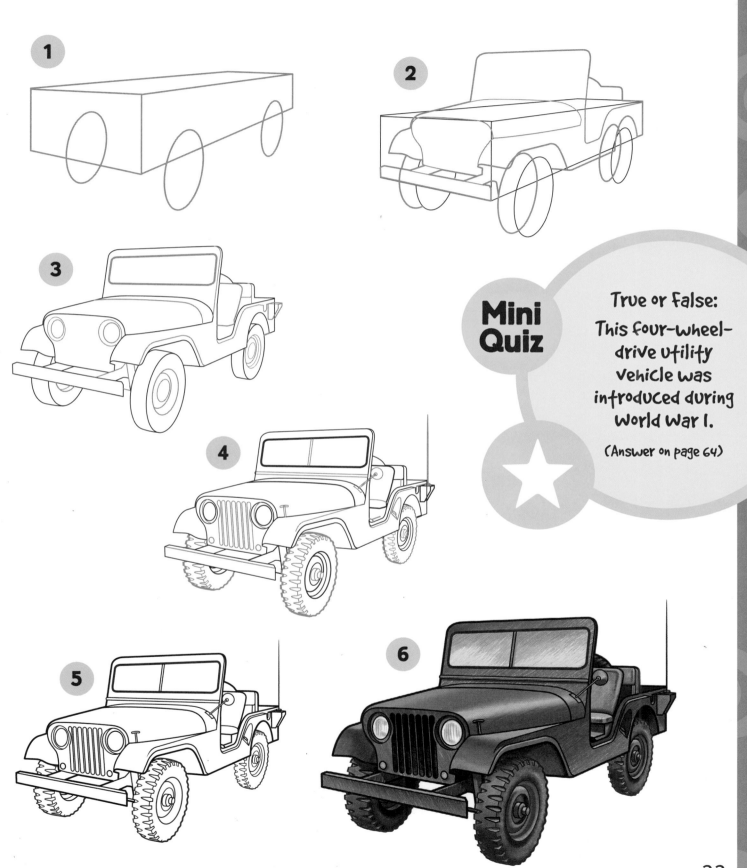

Mini Quiz

True or false:
This four-wheel-drive utility vehicle was introduced during World War I.

(Answer on page 64)

M36 Tank Destroyer

Did You Know?

The original tank destroyers had an open turret or a rotating weapon platform on top of the tank. Modern tanks feature covered turrets.

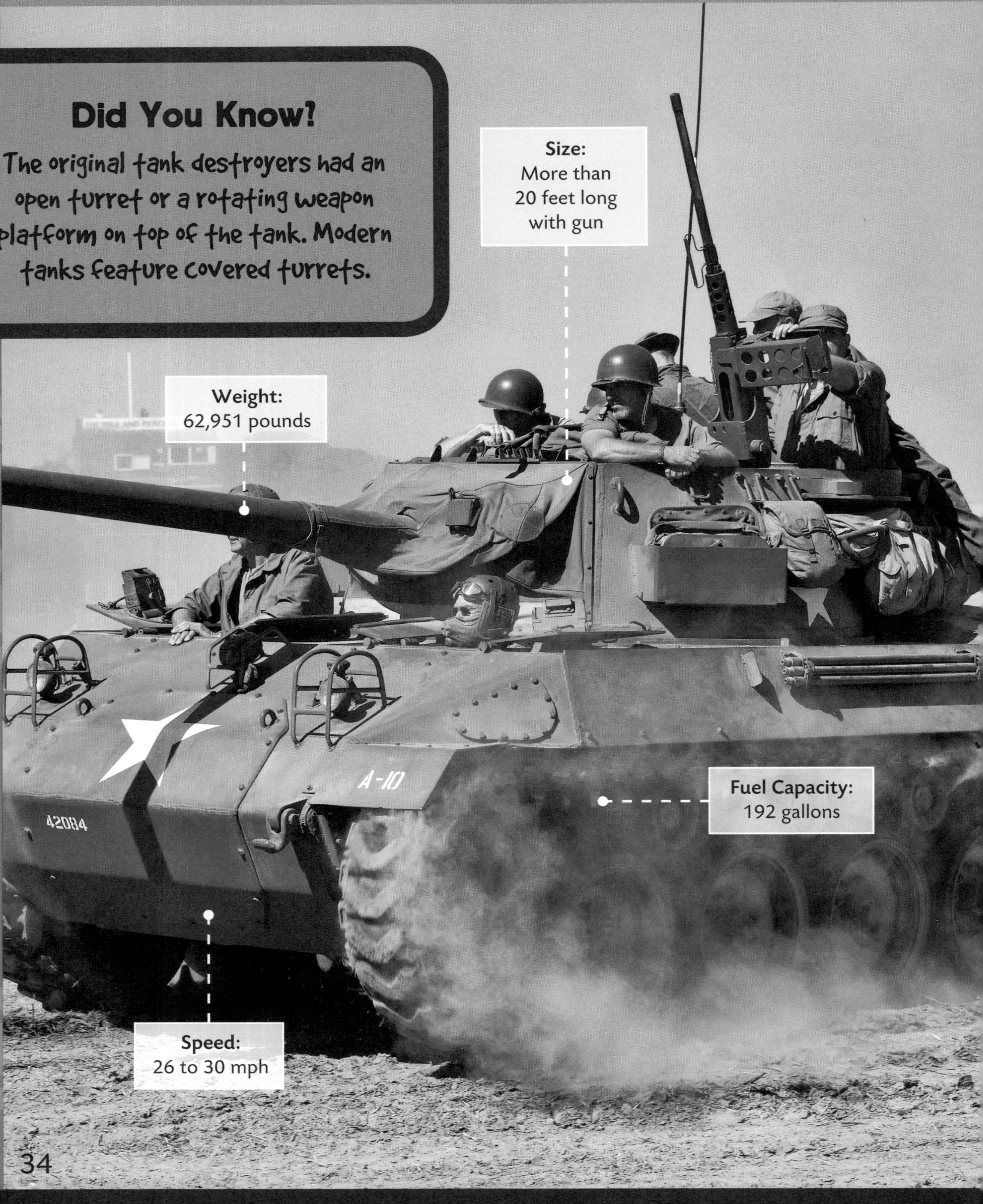

Size: More than 20 feet long with gun

Weight: 62,951 pounds

Fuel Capacity: 192 gallons

Speed: 26 to 30 mph

Used in WWII, the M36 featured an anti-tank gun that could destroy other tanks up to 10 miles away.

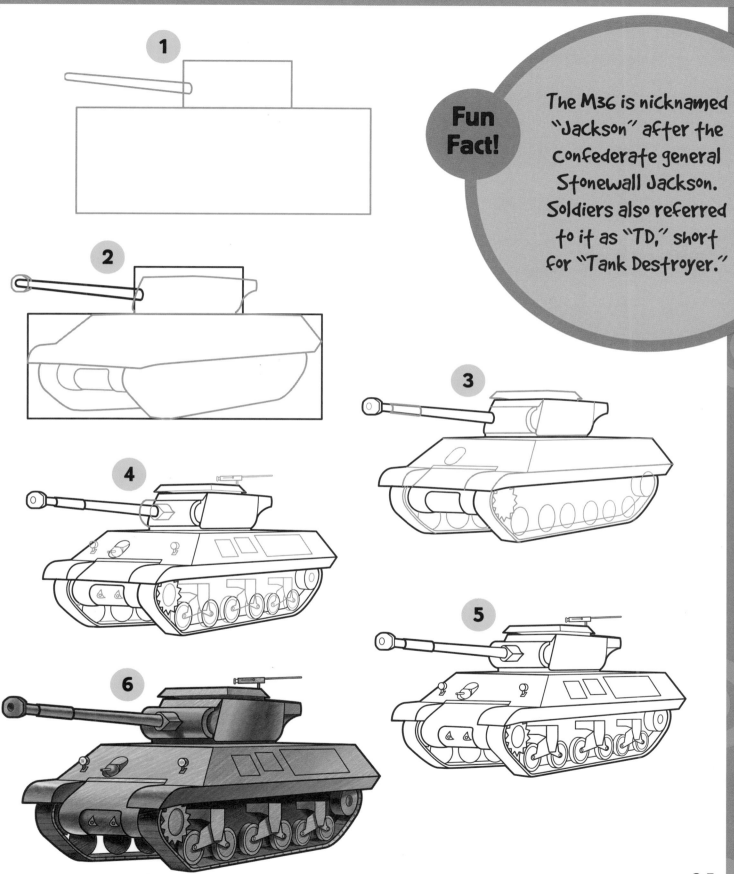

Fun Fact!

The M36 is nicknamed "Jackson" after the Confederate general Stonewall Jackson. Soldiers also referred to it as "TD," short for "Tank Destroyer."

F-16

Details

Size: 49 feet, 5 inches long
Weight: 19,700 pounds
Fuel Capacity: More than 1,000 gallons with the ability to hold external tanks
Speed: 1,500 mph

Did You Know?

There are about 1,500 F-16 jets currently in service with the United States Air Force.

This single-engine, single-pilot fighter jet is small, light, quick, and it flies at supersonic, neck-breaking speeds!

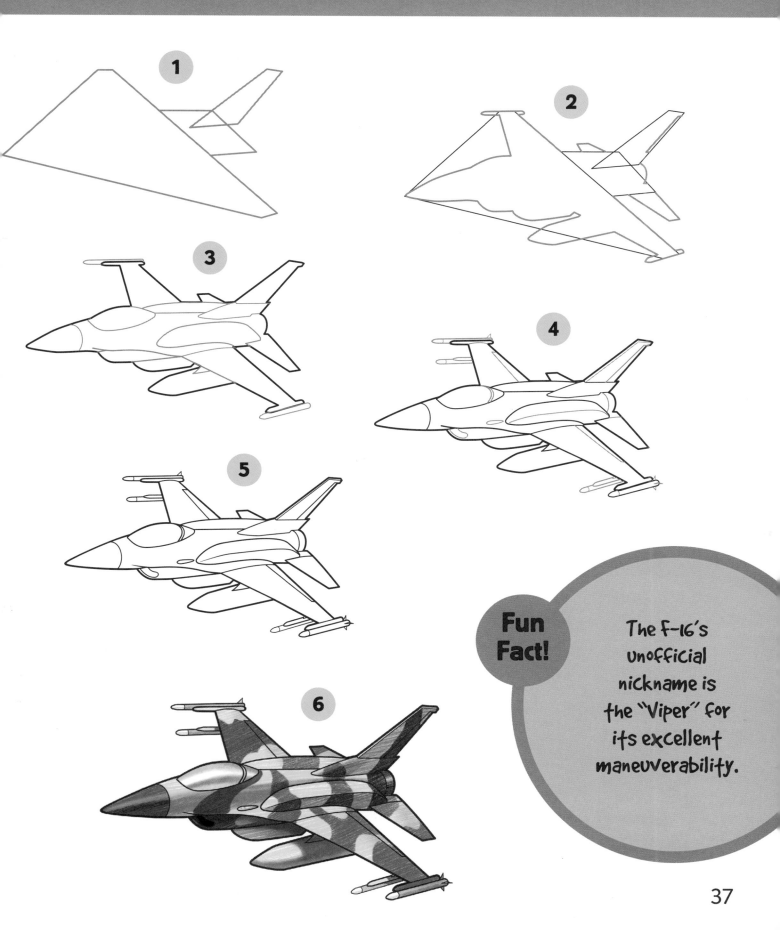

1

2

3

4

5

6

Fun Fact! The F-16's unofficial nickname is the "Viper" for its excellent maneuverability.

Lightweight Twin-Engine Helicopter

Did You Know?

The first successful helicopter flight occurred in 1939.

This sharp-looking chopper seats six passengers and two pilots. Its fast engine can even overtake speedboats.

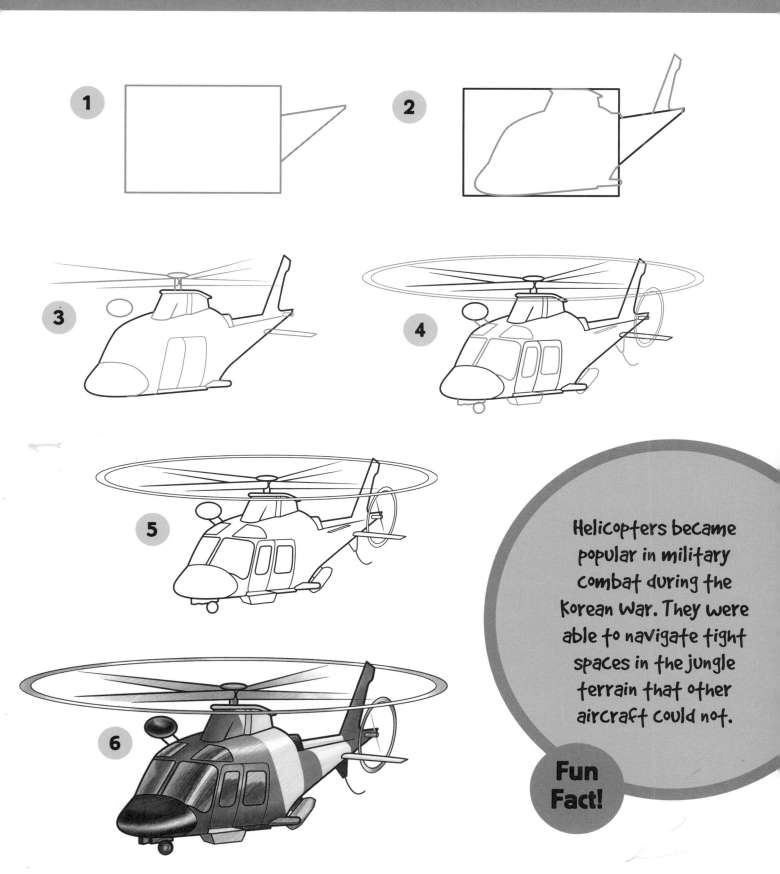

Helicopters became popular in military combat during the Korean War. They were able to navigate tight spaces in the jungle terrain that other aircraft could not.

Fun Fact!

Twin-Engine Military Hovercraft

Details

Size: 15 to 40 feet long
Weight: 650 to 2,000 pounds
Fuel Capacity: 16 gallons with the ability to hold external tanks
Speed: 40 mph on smooth water, 17 mph on land

Did You Know?

A hovercraft is operated by a pilot as an aircraft, not by a captain as a ship!

This rectangular craft can jet across ice, snow, and water. It uses high-speed fans to create an air cushion underneath its rubber sides—it literally floats on air!

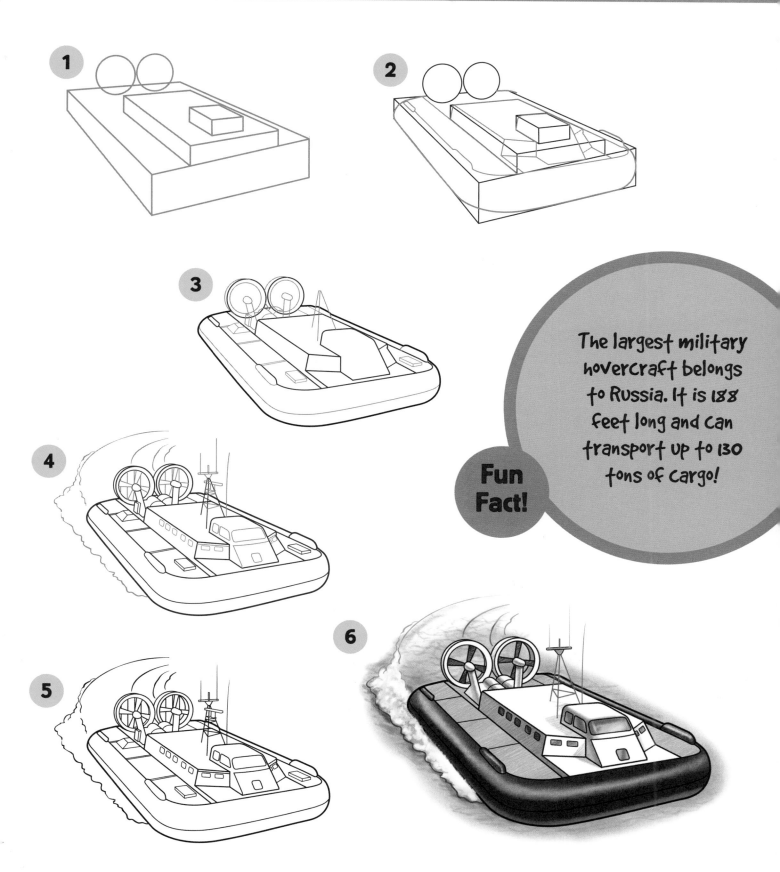

The largest military hovercraft belongs to Russia. It is 188 feet long and can transport up to 130 tons of cargo!

Fun Fact!

Medium-Lift Transport Helicopter

Did You Know?

The United States Navy used this helicopter before the Air Force. The Air Force operated several of the Navy's version of the helicopter and eventually designed its own modification.

Size:
73 feet long

Speed:
140 to 165 mph

Weight:
13,000 pounds

Fuel Capacity:
More than 650 gallons

This twin-engine chopper can be modified to perform many different tasks, including helping to fight fires!

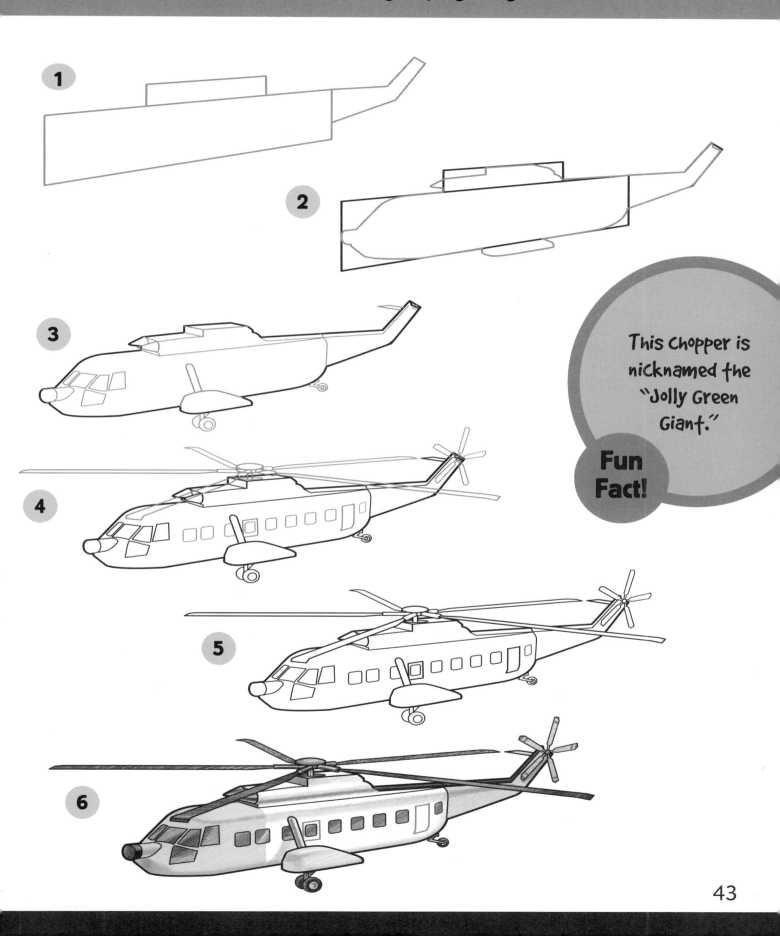

This chopper is nicknamed the "Jolly Green Giant."

Fun Fact!

High Mobility Multipurpose Wheeled Vehicle (HMMWV)

Did You Know?

There are almost 20 variants of the HMMWV in service with the United States Armed forces.

Weight:
5,000 to 10,000 pounds

Size:
16 feet long

Speed:
70 mph

Fuel Capacity:
25 gallons

Before it became a consumer sport-utility vehicle, this diesel-fueled machine was used for military purposes.

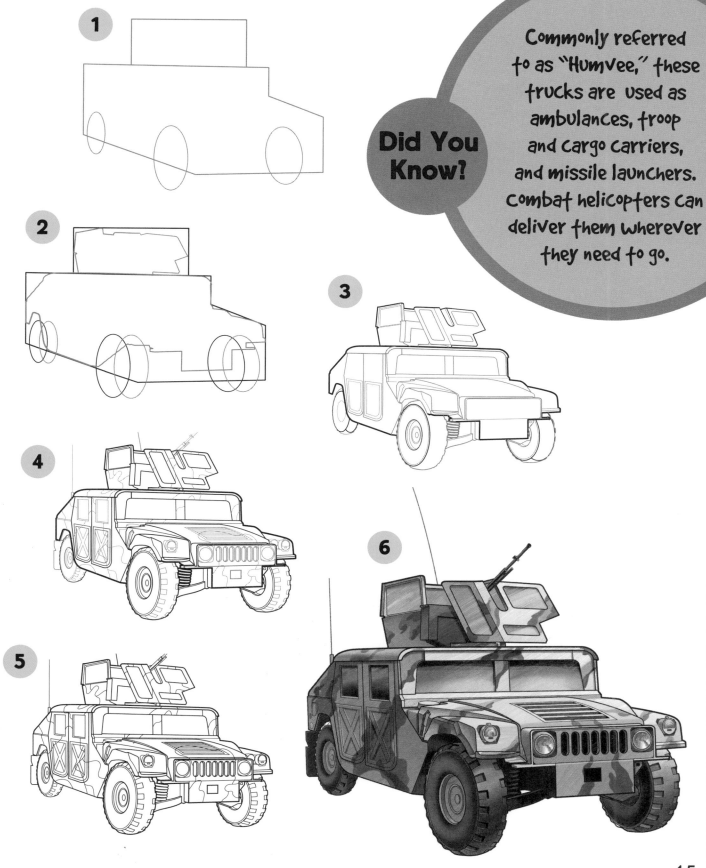

Did You Know?

Commonly referred to as "Humvee," these trucks are used as ambulances, troop and cargo carriers, and missile launchers. Combat helicopters can deliver them wherever they need to go.

Stealth Fighter Jet

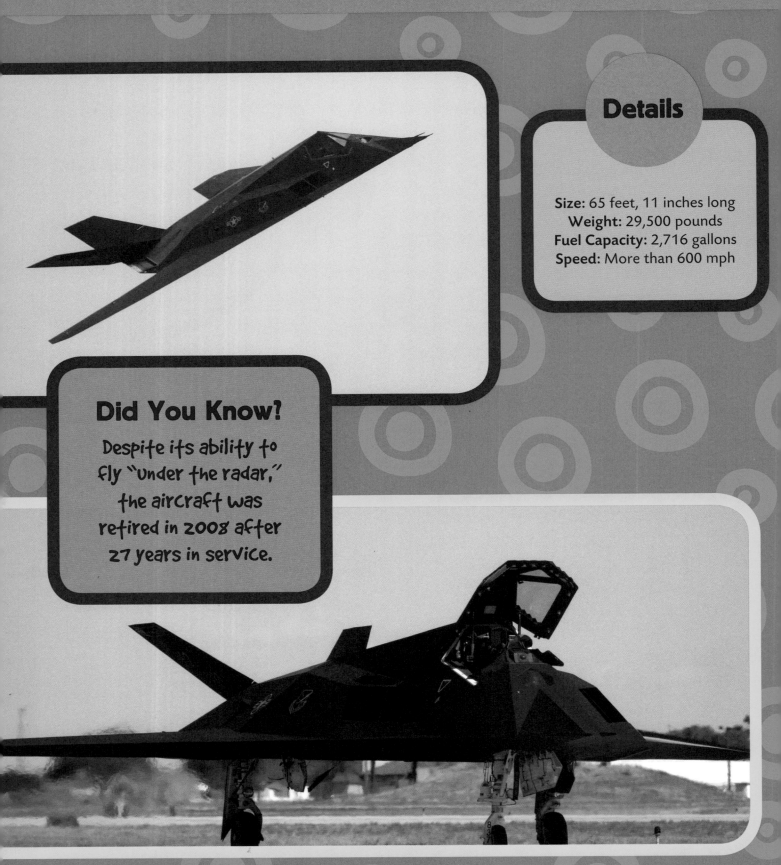

Details

Size: 65 feet, 11 inches long
Weight: 29,500 pounds
Fuel Capacity: 2,716 gallons
Speed: More than 600 mph

Did You Know?

Despite its ability to fly "under the radar," the aircraft was retired in 2008 after 27 years in service.

This sneak-attack jet may look bizarre, but its triangular shape helped it escape radar detection.

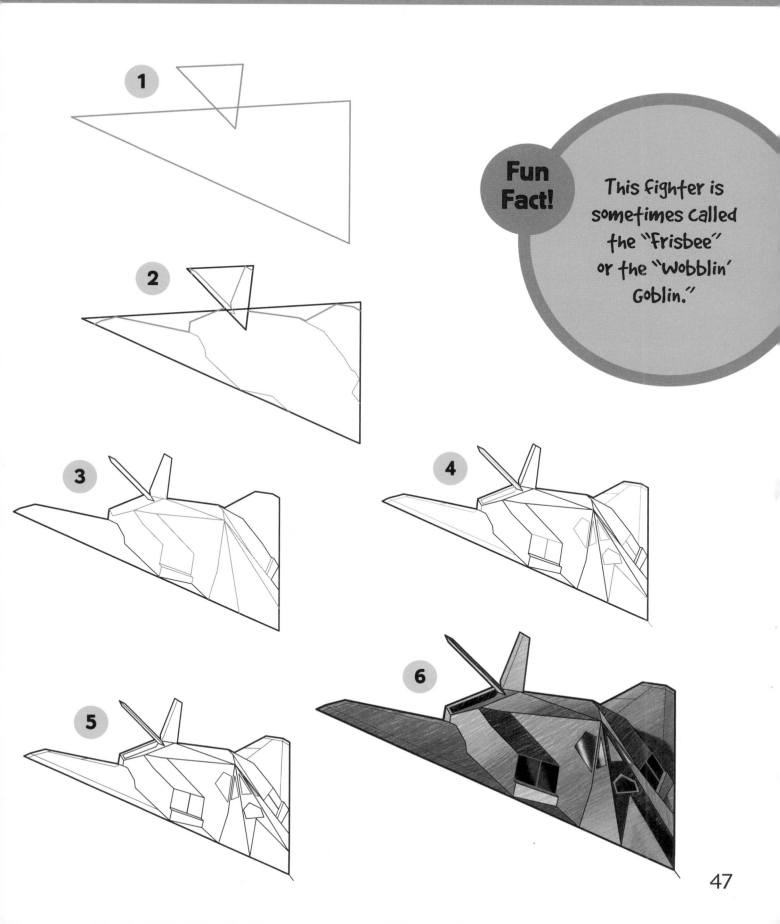

Fun Fact!

This fighter is sometimes called the "Frisbee" or the "Wobblin' Goblin."

F-14

Details

Size: 62 feet, 9 inches long
Weight: 43,600 pounds
Fuel Capacity: About 2,400 gallons with the ability to hold external tanks
Speed: 1,544 mph

Did You Know?

The F-14 can attack six targets at once. It's even capable of shooting down another fighter plane or a cruise missile.

This fighter jet can carry up to 13,000 pounds of missiles. At the touch of a button, the pilot can change the angle of its wings to make it fly faster or slower.

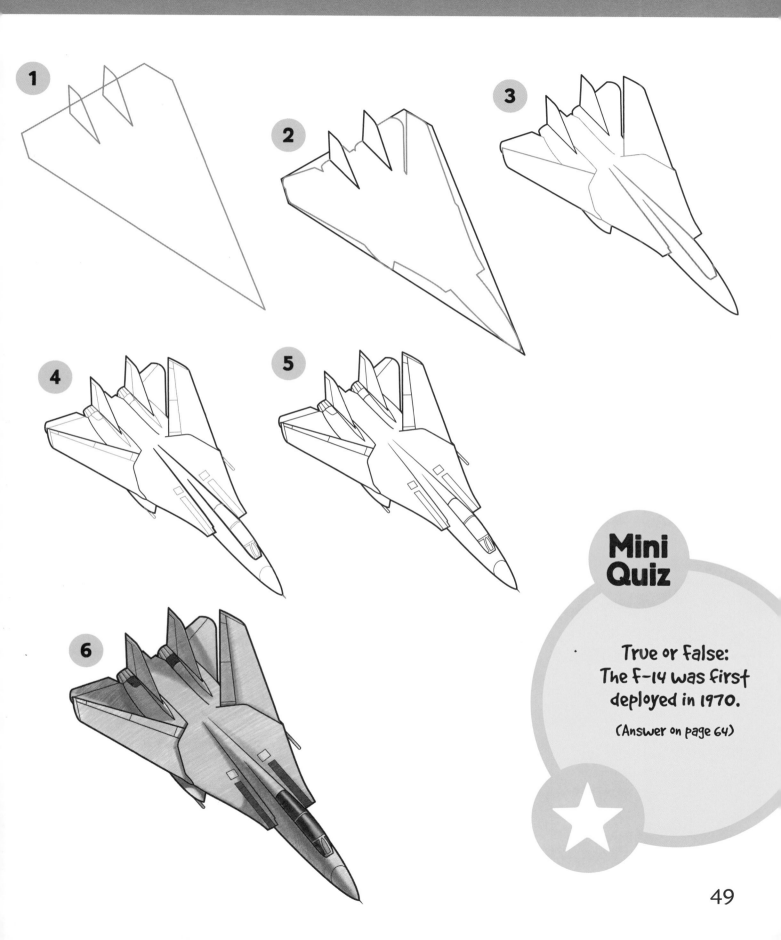

Mini Quiz

True or false:
The F-14 was first
deployed in 1970.

(Answer on page 64)

Guided Missile Submarine

Size:
560 feet long

Speed:
23 to 29 mph

Weight:
16,765 tons

Did You Know?

While the actual depth is classified, United States Navy submarines can submerge at least 800 feet.

This ferocious vessel runs on nuclear power. It can carry 154 land-attack cruise missiles or 24 nuclear warheads.

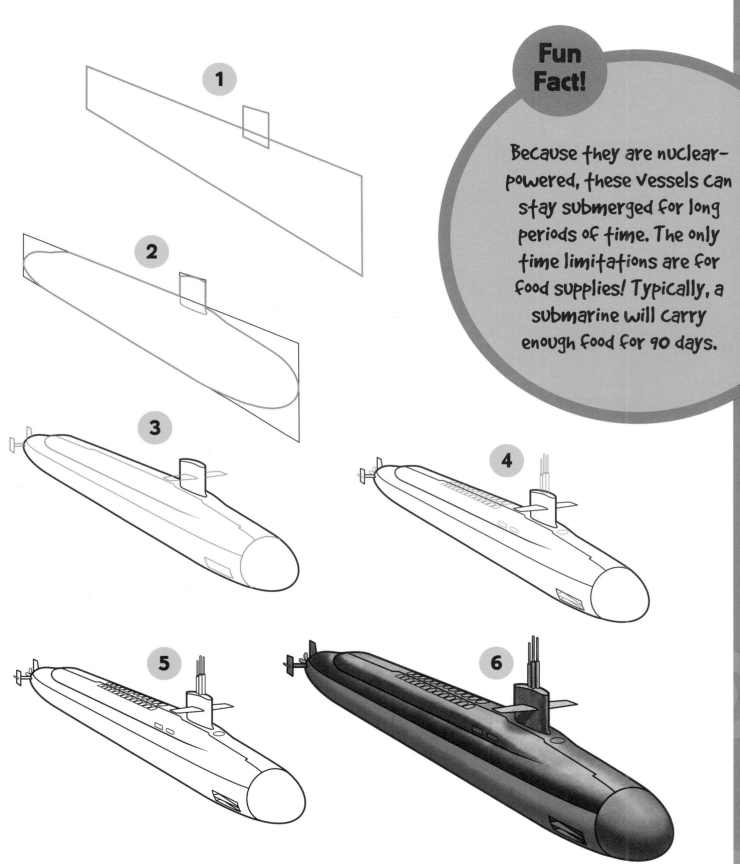

Fun Fact!

Because they are nuclear-powered, these vessels can stay submerged for long periods of time. The only time limitations are for food supplies! Typically, a submarine will carry enough food for 90 days.

Tilt-Rotor Vertical/Short Takeoff & Landing Aircraft

Speed:
310 mph

Size:
57 feet,
4 inches long

Fuel Capacity:
2,040 gallons

Weight:
More than
33,000 pounds

Fun Fact!

This helicopter can do things planes only dream about. Like a helicopter, it can carry up to 15,000 pounds of cargo on two external hooks, and it can take off and land without a runway. Like a plane, it's able to cruise 30,000 feet above sea level for more than 2,000 miles without refueling!

The bulky gray aircraft is a real-life transformer: it can turn itself into an airplane AND a helicopter.

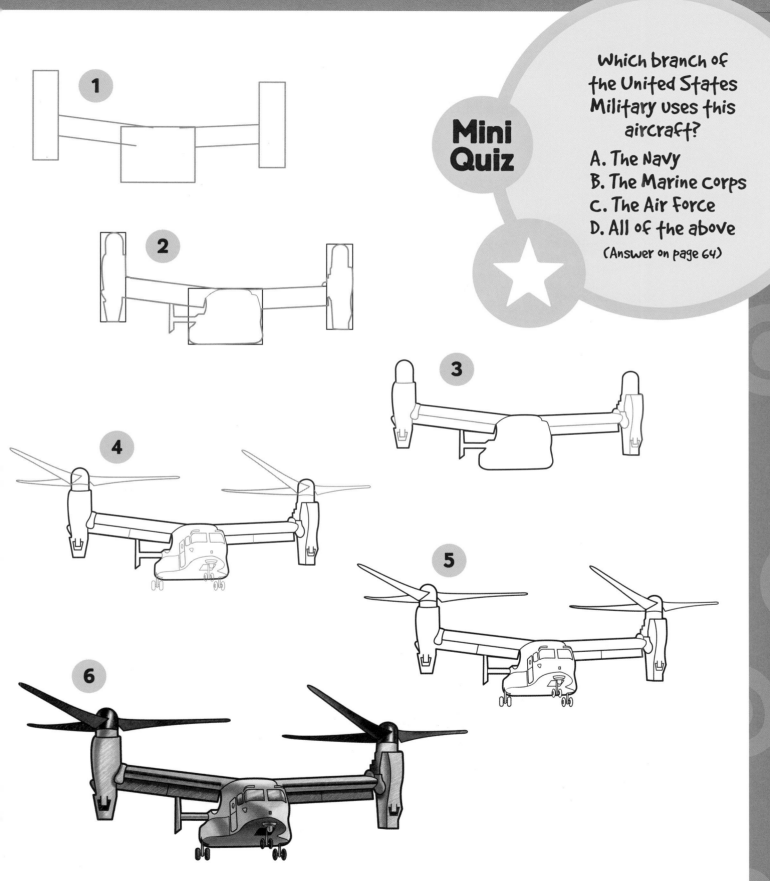

Mini Quiz

Which branch of the United States Military uses this aircraft?

A. The Navy
B. The Marine Corps
C. The Air Force
D. All of the above

(Answer on page 64)

53

Maritime Patrol Aircraft

Details

Size: 80 feet, 3 inches long
Weight: 24,250 pounds
Fuel Capacity:
More than 2,000 gallons
Speed: 300 mph

Did You Know?

This plane can hold up to 71 combat-ready troops or about 20,000 pounds of cargo.

This multipurpose plane is often used for search and rescue missions, as well as a variety of other functions.

Fun Fact!

This aircraft can be fitted with an Airborne Warning and Control System (AWACS) rotodome.

Nuclear-Powered Supercarrier

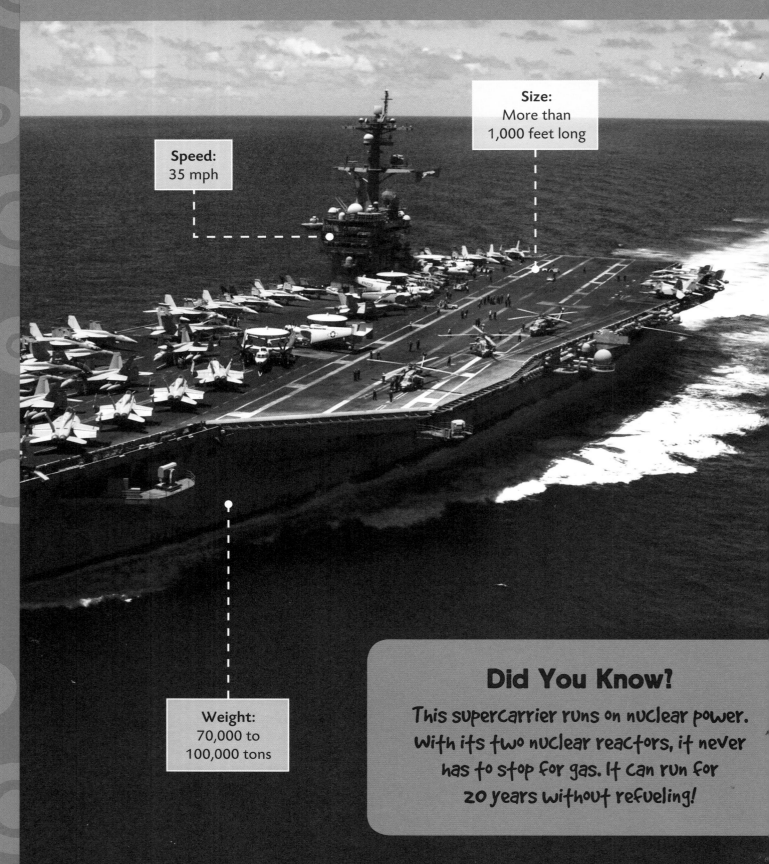

Speed:
35 mph

Size:
More than
1,000 feet long

Weight:
70,000 to
100,000 tons

Did You Know?

This supercarrier runs on nuclear power. With its two nuclear reactors, it never has to stop for gas. It can run for 20 years without refueling!

This enormous ship is used as a portable flight deck for up to 85 airplanes. Its flat deck is also a giant runway.

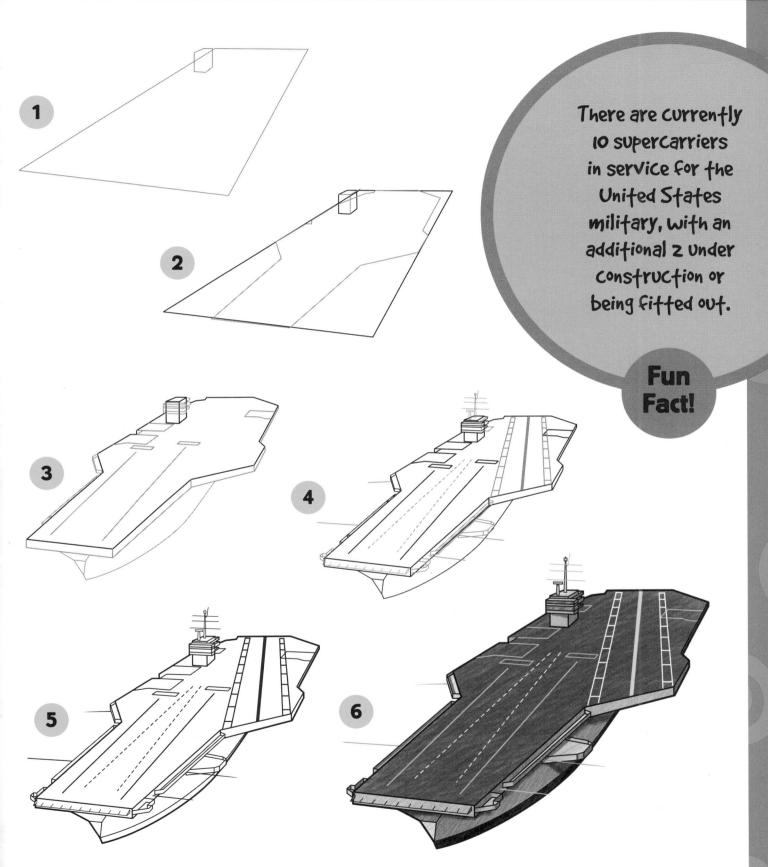

1

2

3

4

5

6

There are currently 10 supercarriers in service for the United States military, with an additional 2 under construction or being fitted out.

Fun Fact!

Heavy Expanded Mobility Tactical Truck (HEMTT)

Details

Size: 34 feet long
Weight: 30,000 to 50,000 pounds
Fuel Capacity: 155 gallons
Speed: 57 mph

Did You Know?

More than 27,000 HEMTTs have been produced.

Nicknamed the "dragon wagon," this eight-wheel diesel truck can carry supplies, fuel tanks, and large artillery.

1

2

3

4

Mini Quiz

How much weight can this vehicle carry?

A. 1 ton
B. 5 tons
C. 10 tons
D. 12 tons

(Answer on page 64)

5

6

Research Vessel

Size: 200 to 270 feet long
Weight: 2,500 to 3,500 tons
Fuel Capacity: More than 200,000 gallons
Speed: 12 mph to 17 mph

Did You Know?

The United States Navy uses research vessels to detect submarines and mines and to test new sonar and weapons. Some of the vessels are also leased to different oceanography institutions for scientific research.

This powerful ship rams through ice up to 6 feet thick! Its steel hull acts like a sledgehammer, floating up onto ice and crushing it with a 13,000-ton weight.

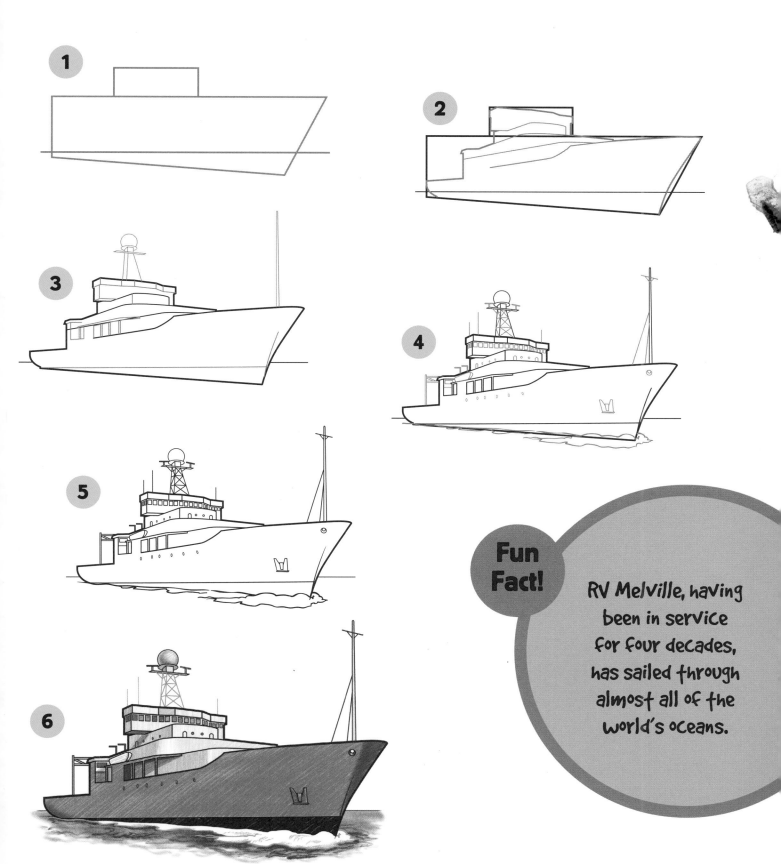

Fun Fact!

RV Melville, having been in service for four decades, has sailed through almost all of the world's oceans.

Search and Rescue (SAR) Helicopter

Size:
44 feet,
6 inches long

Speed:
125 mph

Fuel Capacity:
61 gallons

Weight:
About 5,000
pounds

Did You Know?

There are currently several varieties of SAR helicopters in active service, with a combined total of more than 100 units in use by the United States Coast Guard.

This chopper sports a watertight hull, allowing it to land on water. It is frequently used to rescue people at sea.

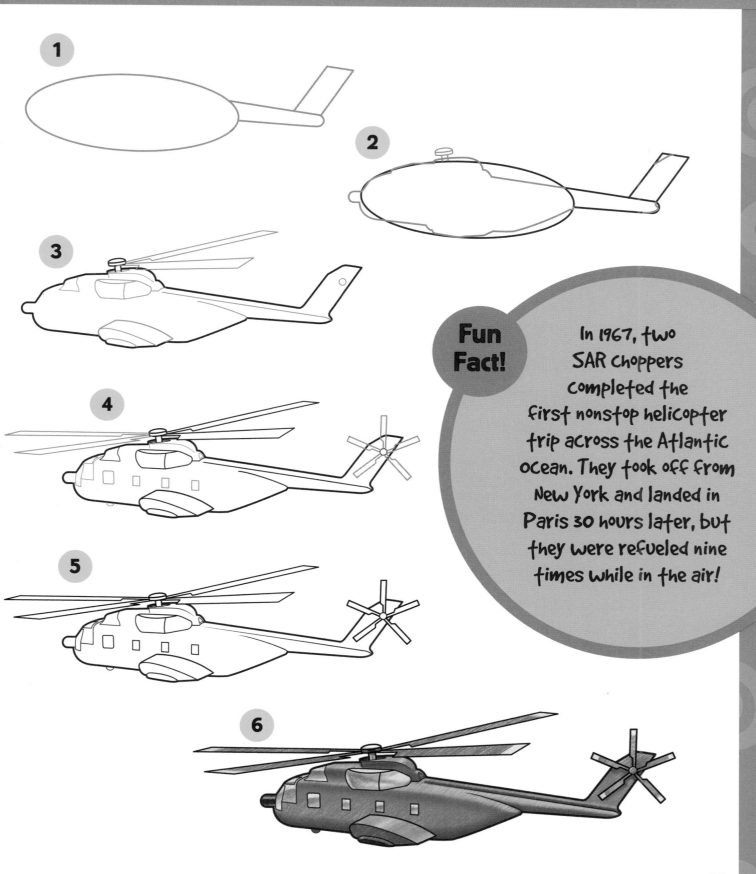

Fun Fact!

In 1967, two SAR choppers completed the first nonstop helicopter trip across the Atlantic ocean. They took off from New York and landed in Paris 30 hours later, but they were refueled nine times while in the air!

Mini Quiz Answers

Page 13: C. A modern AWACS can detect aircraft from up to 250 miles away.

Page 17: A. The B-52 bomber can carry up to 70,000 pounds of bombs.

Page 19: True. Since their debut in 1978, Black Hawk helicopters have flown a combined 4 million hours.

Page 23: C. It cost 50 million dollars to build the Sea Shadow.

Page 27: B. The M113 can carry 11 passengers, one driver, and one track commander.

Page 33: False. The vehicle was introduced during World War II.

Page 49: False. The F-14 was first deployed in 1974.

Page 53: D. The Navy, Marine Corps, and Air Force all use this aircraft.

Page 59: C. This monstrous vehicle can carry up to 10 tons of cargo.